C000186414

CHICHESTER
PAST AND PRESENT

Compiled and photographed
by
KENNETH GREEN

MILESTONE PUBLICATIONS

Published by Milestone Publications,
62 Murray Road, Horndean, Hampshire PO8 9JL

British Library Cataloguing in Publication Data

Green, Kenneth
    Chichester past and present.
    1. Chichester (West Sussex) — History —
    Pictorial works   2. Chichester (West Sussex)
    — Description — Views
    I. Title
    942.2'62   DA690.C53

ISBN 0-903852-94-2

Design Brian Iles

Typeset by Monitor Publications Ltd, Hayling Island

Printed and bound in Great Britain by
R.J. Acford, Chichester, W. Sussex

Jacket front: East Street , 1912
Jacket rear: A carriage and pair waiting outside the
Buttermarket, North Street, 1896

ACKNOWLEDGEMENTS

Until I took on the task of preparing this work I did not
appreciate how much the compiler of such publications
has to rely on the help and generosity of others. I wish
to thank all who have helped, in particular the staff of
Whitbys, for advice and help with photographs; Pat and
Alison Combes, Wally Dew, Peter Dunnaway, Colin
Harmsworth, Sheila and Leslie Holden, Albert Sivyer and
Malcolm Summers for lending me pictures from their
collections; Rosemary Gilmour and Ann Bone of the
Chichester District Museum and to the Local Studies
section, which we are so lucky to have, in the County
Library for their help.

To Kath Riley for typing and to many others who
confirmed dates and other information. Thanks must also
go to Nicholas Pine of Milestone Publications for
suggesting the book and giving me the opportunity to
undertake it and finally, and especially to my wife, Sheila,
for her help and encouragement.

INTRODUCTION

Over the years there have been many books written about Chichester. In the late 1950's the City Council, with commendable foresight, sponsored a series of booklets dealing with various aspects of the city's history.

More recently, Bernard Price has produced three books which cover the progress of Chichester during the last century.

In *Chichester Past and Present* we have set out to show the changes that have taken place in the street scene during the time in which photography has been available.

The book's format is one that has proved most popular, the juxtaposition of old pictures with photographs taken at, or as near as is possible, the same place today.

Chichester is an ancient city, founded as a garrison by the Romans. Little is known of the Saxon period, although by the ninth century, Chichester must have been of some importance as the city boasted its own mint.

Soon after the Norman conquest, Chichester became a cathedral city when the Bishopric was transferred from Selsey. In Medieval times, Chichester had not one but two hospitals, plus monasteries for the Black and the Grey friars. The chapel of the latter can still be seen and is pictured in this book.

The visual centre of Chichester, the city cross, was built in 1501. Trade was picking up, and 70 years later some 140 vessels were based at the port of Chichester.

In the Civil War of 1642, Chichester was beseiged by Parliamentary troops under the command of Sir William Waller. After a few days, the city fell, and troops rampaged through the streets. The cathedral was desecrated; pictures, stained glass windows and tombs were damaged, the organ and much of the panelling destroyed.

Elsewhere in the city, the devastation was considerable. The almost complete destruction of the St. Pancras district essentially put an end to an unusual local industry, that of needle-making.

The golden age of Chichester was undoubtedly the 150 years from 1720. The city was then the centre of the local corn and wool trade, and was the administrative and legal centre of Sussex, returning two members of parliament.

Indeed one of the MPs for Chichester, William Huskisson became the first person in Britain to be killed in a railway accident.

This was a time of much new building, and many of the old timber buildings were rebuilt in brick; even today, Chichester can aptly be described as a Georgian city.

The Chichester Ship Canal was opened in 1822, but soon ceased to be used commercially when the railway arrived in 1846.

The city's population increased dramatically from 4200 in 1780 to more than double (8500) a century later. Today Chichester has some 30,000 residents.

The city's churches could no longer meet the needs of their increased congregations and the early half of the nineteenth century saw the building of several new places of worship. Providence Chapel was built in 1809, St. John's

Church in 1812 and in 1832 St. Bartholomews was rebuilt.

The consecration of St. Paul's Church in 1836 was the first duty of Bishop Wm. Otter and in 1848 the new St. Peter the Great Church opened, its congregation having worshipped previously in an aisle in the Cathedral. The Roman Catholic Church in Southgate was built in 1855.

The period also saw the establishment of schools in the city and in 1839 the Theological College was established — followed in the next year by the Bishop Otter College, originally to train men as teachers, it later closed and reopened as a ladies training college. Other buildings during these years included the Corn Exchange, the Railway Station and the Butter Market.

Gas for lighting came to Chichester in 1823, the Chichester gas works being built by the canal basin in Stockbridge Road, Chichester was one of the first towns to be so served, however other utilities were slow in being provided and it was 1874 before mains water was available. Main drainage did not come until 1894. A private company installed electric lighting in the city in 1909 and was taken over by the Corporation in 1921.

The advent of photography excited the locals. In 1880, the *White Horse* in South Street had a dark room specially built for the use of amateur photographers; nearby, the Sussex School of Photography was taking in students.

At the turn of the century the trades associated with horse-drawn transport were major employers. There were stables, smithies and coachbuilders aplenty, and some of our old pictures show the premises where a horse and carriage could be hired.

With the invention of the internal combustion engine we can see from the photographs that the hotels and inns were quick to offer garaging facilities, usually converting their stables for that purpose.

In 1956, Chichester was chosen, together with Bath, Chester, and York for a government-sponsored conservation study. In recent years, the city centre has been designated a conservation area, which restricts proposals for development within its boundaries.

It is worth mentioning that various groups have been formed, notably the Chichester Society to monitor any proposal for change.

The object of *Chichester Past and Present* is to entertain, but if in so doing, it helps us to appreciate some of what has been lost, then perhaps it will strengthen our resolve to preserve the best of what is left.

Kenneth Green
Chichester, 1986

CONTENTS

North Street	6
North Street	8
North Street	10
Council House, North Street	12
North Street	14
Northgate	16
Northgate	18
Northgate	20
St Pauls Church	22
Royal West Sussex Hospital	24
Chichester Barracks	26
Washington Street	28
The Avenue Summersdale	30
The North Walls	32
Tower Street	34
Belltower from Tower Street	36
West Street	38
West Street	40
West Street	42
Westgate	44
Westgate	46
Main Road, Fishbourne	48
South Street	50
The Post Office, South Street	52
South Street	54
Southgate	56
Chichester Railway Station	58
Stockbridge Road	60
Chichester Canal	62
The Market Cross	64
The Royal Arms, East Street	66
The Cross from East Street	68
East Street	70
East Street	72
East Street	74
Corn Exchange, Baffins Lane	76
East Street	78
Eastgate	80
Eastgate Square	82
Eastgate Square	84
The Hornet	86
Greyfriars Chapel	88
St. Pancras	90
Somerstown	92

NORTH STREET 1885 In this, one of the earliest photographs of Chichester Streets, can be seen The Wheatsheaf Hotel, a notorious Chichester drinking house and a favourite of soldiers from The Barracks. It was often the scene of fighting and brawling.

NORTH STREET 1986 Above the shopfronts there has been little change in a hundred years. St. Olaves Church is now the S.P.C.K. Bookshop. The Butcher's Shop has shared the fate of many premises in the city and is now a Building Society Office.

7

NORTH STREET 1932 Mention Bull's shop to any old Cicestrian and they will remember with affection the shop that seemed to sell everything. The assistants placed ones money and bill into a wooden ball which rolled via a series of ceiling level tracks to the cashier who sat in a high desk. The receipt and change were returned by the same method.

8

NORTH STREET 1986 When Bulls closed in 1949 the premises were taken over by Perrings until 1955 when Shirley Brothers moved in. The building was destroyed by a fire in 1974, one of several serious fires that have taken place in the city in recent years. These premises are now occupied by Dorothy Perkins.

NORTH STREET 1896 Although I have been unable to discover the occasion of the photograph which I found among plates in the collection of Chichester District Museum, it seems worth including. The band is obviously military. Note the bats and wickets sign over the premises on the right which apparently offers 'Hot and Cold Baths'.

NORTH STREET 1986 Nikolaus Pevsner described North Street as being 'the perfect street of an English county town'. In this picture most of the buildings in the 1896 photograph can still be identified, this part of North Street is mainly devoted to shopping and the advantages of pedestrianisation can clearly be seen.

THE COUNCIL HOUSE NORTH STREET 1906 In North Street there can be seen the work of five men who were among the leading architects of their time. Sir Hugh Casson designed Lennards building in 1961, the Buttermarket was by John Nash in 1908 and Sir Basil Spence was responsible for the Co-op building in 1958.

THE COUNCIL HOUSE 1986 Her Majesty, The Queen had lunch in the Council House on the occasion of her visit to Chichester to distribute the Royal Maundy. The Council House was the work of Roger Morris in 1731 and the 1781 extension by James Wyatt. This picture shows the scaffolding around the building whilst it was being re-roofed.

NORTH STREET 1908 The church to be seen on the left in this picture was that of St.Peter the Less. Built in the 13th Century, it was demolished in 1957. Notice also the gas street lamps, which came to Chichester in 1833, the local residents being proud of the fact that the city was one of the earliest places to have gas lighting.

NORTH STREET 1986 St.Peters is commemorated in the name of the street that has replaced it. The Co-op building on the left was designed by Sir Basil Spence, better known as the Architect of Coventry Cathedral and Sussex University.

NORTHGATE 1930 Micky Guarnaccio was a well known Chichester shopkeeper, he moved out of the premises seen on the left to another shop opposite, this building was demolished shortly after this picture was taken to become Reeds Garage. Mrs Day's Fish and Chip shop was on this site for over sixty years.

NORTHGATE 1986 Sydney Bastow's Pharmacy had occupied a site near the Cross since early in the century. Its present owner Timothy Bastow, moved to Northgate in 1985 when the Fish and Chip Shop closed. Reeds Garage has been converted into a shopping arcade with a distinctive entrance.

NORTHGATE 1961 This picture was taken by Leslie Holden who has represented Chichester West on the District Council since 1979 and is one of the few people who have made a photographic record of the city. This building was for many years the Northgate Fruit Stores, and later T.C. Daniels, Electricians.

NORTHGATE 1986 The building that has replaced the one seen in the earlier picture is one of the less attractive additions to the city in recent years. When it was built, a 4th Century Roman coin and some of the foundations of the old city wall were excavated.

NORTHGATE 1961 These buildings were the premises of Henry Slaney who had occupied them since the 1920s, originally described as a tinsmith who would repair stoves and other household articles, he moved on to the developing need for car body repairs. The buildings were demolished soon after this photograph was taken.

NORTHGATE 1986 Metropolitan Pension Association had been looking for new premises and were offered the Northgate site. They moved in in 1967. Their building is not to everyone's taste but they excuse themselves by blaming the planners who insisted that the building matched the Fire Station built the year before.

ST PAULS CHURCH 1930 St Pauls Church was built in 1836 to meet the 'population explosion' of the early 19th Century. It served the largest Parish in the city for many years, its congregation being swelled by having the barracks within its boundaries.

ST PAULS CHURCH 1986 The church that lost its tower, also its railings and a large part of the churchyard, given up to the Ring Road. The Tower became dangerous and was 'reduced' in 1953. The parish was united with that of St. Peters in 1981.

THE ROYAL WEST SUSSEX HOSPITAL 1918 The hospital opened as the Chichester Infirmary in 1826. The lane behind the hospital is still known as Infirmary Terrace. The hospital was extended and modernised as a memorial to Edward VII in 1913 and in August of that year King George V visited Chichester and gave the hospital its royal status.

24

THE ROYAL WEST SUSSEX HOSPITAL 1986 The hospital has closed; it is still used as administrative offices by the Local Health Authority. St.Richards Hospital in Spitalfields Lane opened in 1937 and when it was enlarged to a District Hospital in 1972, it became known as the Royal West Sussex Hospital (St. Richards) to perpetrate the name.

CHICHESTER BARRACKS 1904 The Military have had a garrison here since 1770. Much of the barracks was built in 1803 to house prisoners from the Napoleonic wars. In 1904 when this picture was taken, it was the Headquarters of the Royal Sussex Regiment.

CHICHESTER BARRACKS 1986 The Royal Sussex was amalgamated with others to form The Queens Regiment in 1966, today the barracks is the home of the Royal Military Police Training School. Whereas the walls were, in 1904, there to keep the soldiers in, the highly sophisticated security is now intended to keep intruders out.

27

WASHINGTON STREET 1945 This picture was taken at the time when the street was celebrating victory at the end of the war. The iron railings fronting the gardens were removed to be melted down to help in the war effort.

28

WASHINGTON STREET 1986 Whereas in 1945 most of the properties were occupied by tenants. Washington Street has now become a very sought after place to live. Unfortunately the houses were built in an age when the need for car parking was not envisaged.

THE AVENUE SUMMERSDALE 1920 Summersdale was an area of Chichester that was built at the turn of the century by Mr. Charles Stride. Avenue Road as it was first called, was to provide homes for the professional men of Chichester. In the street directory of the time of this photograph are listed one Admiral, a General and a couple of Majors.

THE AVENUE SUMMERSDALE 1986 In recent years Summersdale has been developed and the Avenue is no longer a secluded backwater. However the houses are still among the most desirable in the city.

THE NORTH WALLS 1911 The city walls were first built by the Romans and strengthened in Saxon times. Records show that they have required constant maintenance ever since. The Elm trees were planted in 1720 by the Mayor, William Costello.

THE NORTH WALLS 1986 The Grange and the buildings in the 1911 picture were demolished to enable an extension to the County Hall to be built; it houses the design staff of the County Council. The walls remain a popular walk for Cicestrians and it is hoped to open up access to even more of their length.

TOWER STREET 1913 The Bell Tower dominates this view of the street; the gateway on the right led to The Grange, the house of Ebenezer Prior, the last of Chichester's woolstaplers and a former Mayor of the city.

TOWER STREET 1986 The cottages have gone and have been replaced with flats and maisonettes. On the right is the County Library building which was completed in 1967. It stands on the site of The Ship Public house which dated back to 1784.

THE BELLTOWER FROM TOWER STREET 1904 On the left of the picture can be seen the premises of Mr. W.E. Smith, described as a 'Fly Proprietor' (a small horse-drawn carriage). The next building housed the 'March Charity for supplying sick poor with domestic comforts'.

THE BELLTOWER FROM TOWER STREET 1986 Although there seems little change to the buildings externally, inside is the sales area of The Army and Navy Department Store. The Scaffolding on the Cathedral has been a constant feature over the last ten years.

WEST STREET 1908 Both the Dolphin and the Anchor Hotels can now be seen to be advertising garage facilities. The man with the peg leg was Walter Bridger who besides being the gate keeper at Fishbourne level crossing was also a Sunday School teacher, not averse to using his 'leg' to correct misbehaving pupils.

WEST STREET 1986 The Dolphin and Anchor Hotels amalgamated in 1910 and are now part of the Trust House Forte Group. With the exception of buses and the disabled this part of the street is no longer open to motor vehicles.

WEST STREET 1932 Many will remember the Southdown Bus Company's offices when they were in West Street, conveniently Miss Nan Durtnell had her tea rooms on the upper floor. Behind the trees where the Post Office now is was the house of Dr.Arthur Barford, Physician, Surgeon and Medical Officer of Health for the city.

WEST STREET 1986 The Post Office was built in 1937 and although the Bus Station moved to Southgate in 1953 the buses still stop in West Street. They are among the few vehicles allowed to enter the pedestrianised centre of the city.

WEST STREET 1907 Towering over the houses can be seen the spire of the Cathedral, many of the residents at this time could still remember the old spire falling on the 21st of February 1861, and the new spire being completed in 1866.

WEST STREET 1986 This picture demonstrates how little some parts of the city have changed. However whereas the houses in the picture of 1907 were private residences, today they are principally offices or professional consulting rooms. The stone built building in the centre of both pictures is the Prebendal School, founded in the 13th Century.

WESTGATE 1963 Taken just as the demolition men were moving in as the buildings had become a bottleneck for traffic. Before the by pass was opened in 1937 this road had been the A27 coastal trunk road. The small building on the left had been the old toll house, for many years, Charlie Hooker's sweet and confectionary shop.

44

WESTGATE 1986 The ring road and the roundabout that replaced the old buildings have undoubtedly helped the movement of traffic but the character of this part of the city is lost. The Old Toll House has enjoyed several changes of use, it was for a time a 'Poodle Parlour' it is now an Indian Restaurant.

WESTGATE 1914 This road was the main entrance to the city from the West, as can be seen, it was still more suited to horse-drawn traffic than to the motor car.

WESTGATE 1986 Although much widened the street has not changed a great deal. The building in the picture was once the offices of Chichester Tannery, now County Council offices. The building seen has been converted to flats.

MAIN ROAD FISHBOURNE 1910 On the right can be seen the primitive Methodist Chapel, erected in 1872. It had seats for 100 but at its peak only achieved some 32 regular worshippers.

MAIN ROAD FISHBOURNE 1986 The Chapel was closed in 1971 and demolished to form the site for two houses. The building on the left, which has replaced the glasshouse in the 1910 picture, is now the Bric-a-Brac shop of Mr. Les Hickman, a source of much 'Chichesterabilia' for the Author.

49

SOUTH STREET 1924 The building on the left was the office of the West Sussex Gazette which for many years enjoyed the phone number 'Chichester 1', next to it in this picture is the Crown Inn which closed in 1924. On the right next to the White Horse was Turnbulls. Gents Outfitters, the building was demolished in 1964.

50

SOUTH STREET 1986 The White Horse is one of the oldest inns in the city. Records show that in 1643 the Landlord was Thomas Ball, also Mayor of Chichester. Mervyn Cutten, the well known local historian, describes the sign as a travesty of the original, at least the ornate bracket with its gilded grapes has been retained.

THE POST OFFICE — SOUTH STREET 1912 The post office was built in South Street in 1891 and was replaced by the new G.P.O. in West Street in 1937. The premises remained in use as the Sorting Office for Chichester until 1964 when the Basin Road Sorting Offices were built.

FORMER POST OFFICE — SOUTH STREET 1986 When vacated by the Post Office the building was extensively altered by Messrs Whiteheads. Care being taken to preserve the character and proportions of the exterior of the old building. Jack Whitehead set up his business in South Street in 1899.

SOUTH STREET 1947 The church on the left was the Congregational Chapel built in 1882 and demolished in 1980, as can be seen car parking was already becoming a problem in the city.

SOUTH STREET 1986 Just visible on the right is the old Chichester Theatre, it was Lewis's House Furnishers in the 1947 photograph, now it is 'The Old Theatre Mall' another shopping arcade.

55

SOUTHGATE 1950 This picture shows two Chichester landmarks that no longer exist, The County Police Station and the gasometers of the Chichester Gas Company. The police station closed in 1937 with the opening of the new premises in Kingsham Road. During the war years the old police station was occupied by Army units.

SOUTHGATE 1986 The Southdown Bus Company built the new bus station in 1965, and at the same time the bus garage in Basin Road, the latter being one of the largest single span buildings in the country at the time. The demolition of the old police station gave the opportunity for the building of the Southgate circulatory system.

CHICHESTER RAILWAY STATION 1928 The station buildings were erected with the coming of the railway in 1846. Although it is easy to become nostalgic about the old italianesque style structure, there were those who speculated that it had not been painted since then. Towards the end of its days it had become a considerable eyesore.

CHICHESTER RAILWAY STATION 1986 The old station was demolished in 1958 and the present one was opened in 1961, it was built to the design of British Railways Architect's Department which probably says it all.

STOCKBRIDGE ROAD 1911 In this view, from a picture postcard one can see the signal box, from where the level crossing gates were controlled, and the corrugated iron roofed footbridge over the railway line. The cottages were owned by the railway company and were occupied by the signalmen and their families.

STOCKBRIDGE ROAD 1986 The gates have been replaced by barriers controlled electronically with the aid of television cameras from a signal box half a mile away. The old signal box and the cottages have become redundant and have been demolished.

CHICHESTER CANAL 1930 The Canal was opened in 1822. It never reached the level of business hoped for by its promoters and was virtually closed by 1855. In the picture can be seen the chimney and a gasometer of the Chichester Gas Works. The building on the right was the Ice Works.

CHICHESTER CANAL 1986 Where the Gas Works stood is now the G.P.O Sorting Office. Chichester's gas supply now comes from the North Sea. There are plans to develop the Canal's leisure potential.

THE MARKET CROSS 1920 Many of the older residents of the city will remember W.H. Barratts Shop on the corner of the South and West Streets. They were stationers and newsagents, and as can be seen from the painted sign the local agents for Goss china.

THE MARKET CROSS 1986 The Market Cross is Chichester's most famous building. Built in 1501, it was the gift of Edward Storey, Bishop of Chichester. Note the Bishop's mitre, carved in stone, beneath the point of each of the eight arches. Renovated many times over the centuries, little of the original structure now remains.

THE ROYAL ARMS EAST STREET 1906 The Royal Arms is one of the oldest buildings in the city, Tradition has it that John Lumley, Earl of Scarborough, whose house it was, entertained Queen Elizabeth I there in 1591. Other evidence, however, indicates that the present building was not constructed until 1595.

THE ROYAL ARMS 1986 The Inn became known as the Royal Punch House when Queen Victoria expressed her liking for Mr. Hudson's Milk Punch, for which she granted a Royal Warrant in 1840. King Edward VII sampled this brew on a visit to the city in 1904 and a bottle was presented to the Queen on Maundy Thursday 1986.

THE CROSS FROM EAST STREET 1909 A beautiful example of the skill of the Edwardian Photographer who would have produced this picture on a glass plate negative. I believe that the Bell Tower in the background has been erased, probably to give greater clarity to the view of the cross.

THE CROSS FROM EAST STREET 1986 The National Westminster Bank premises replaced buildings that dated back to medieval times. The original Swan Inn, destroyed by fire in 1819, was rebuilt and about 1850 became a shop. Whilst the premises of Richard Edney, house furnishers, it was destroyed by another fire in 1897.

EAST STREET 1908 From medieval times the four main streets of the city have been the centre of trade and activity. The building on the extreme left was Halsteds the ironmongers, they subsequently refronted this shop and the one next to it where to this day their trade mark, a key, can be seen, appropriately on the key stones of the first floor windows.

EAST STREET 1986 This year is the fiftieth anniversary of Marks and Spencers coming to Chichester in 1936, their building of neo georgian design was a better attempt than many at that time to recreate the dominant style of the main streets.

EAST STREET 1920 The shop on the right was that of J.W. Moore, the stationers and printers, the business was later known as Moore and Wingham and since 1946 as Moore and Tillyer, they still occupy the same premises.

EAST STREET 1986 The building that projected over the pavement in the 1920 picture figured in many wedding photographs, it was the Registrar's Office. Sadlers shop which replaced it has been converted to an arcade of small shops, a trend that has been followed by several of the redundant buildings in the city.

East St from Corn Exchange, Chichester

EAST STREET 1921 Pooles pictures were a popular entertainment. My father-in-law remembers, as a boy, climbing up on the corn bins that were around the walls to get a better view of the film being shown. In the distance can be seen a motor works and garage, now the Rediffusion showroom.

74

EAST STREET 1986 The facade of the Corn Exchange has dominated this part of East Street since 1833. Based on the design of a Greek Temple, the building was used for dramatic productions in the early years of the Century and was later converted for use as a cinema.

THE CORN EXCHANGE, BAFFINS LANE 1972 The Corn Exchange was built as a market place for the grain and corn trade in 1833, the cost of £6,000 being met by public subscription. When the front part of the building became used as a cinema, the selling area was transferred to the ground floor of the granary and warehouses seen in this picture.

THE OLD CORN EXCHANGE 1986 When it fell into disuse, the old building was converted into office accommodation. The scheme was carried out with much sensitivity and retains much of the character of the original. The offices are the European Headquarters of John Wiley and Sons the international scientific publishers.

EAST STREET 1907 The large building seen in this picture was the police station, demolished in 1935; a massive iron studded door from one of the cells, with an immense lock with a key 20 inches long was taken to the Guildhall Museum. Opposite is Sharp Garland's shop, at the time of its demolition in 1964 it was the oldest grocery in England.

78

EAST STREET 1986 On the left, Shippams, the most famous of Chichester's businesses. They have caused Chichester Market Cross, their trade mark, to be known throughout the world. The factory was rebuilt in 1912, and received a Royal visit from Queen Mary in 1924. The clock with its wishbone has been a local landmark since the 1930s.

EASTGATE 1911 It became a Chichester tradition to erect replica gates, on the sites of the original city gates, to celebrate Royal occasions. The first were erected for Queen Victoria's Jubilee in 1887. The one shown here was for the Coronation of King George V. Between the gate and the tavern can be seen the doors of the City Fire Brigade.

EASTGATE 1986 Earlier in the year when Chester Kydd renewed their fascia sign, local historians were delighted when the old sign of the Market Tavern was revealed. It has been carefully covered by the new sign, hopefully to be rediscovered by future Cicestrians.

EASTGATE SQUARE 1930 The War Memorial to the 323 Chichester men who fell in the 1914-18 War was unveiled by Field Marshal Sir William Robertson in 1921. The fine chestnut tree seen in the distance is remembered by many Cicestrians.

EASTGATE SQUARE 1986 The memorial, to which the names of the second World War fallen have been added has been moved to the Litten Gardens in St.Pancras. The shops and flats that have recently been completed have been named Sharp Garland House to commemorate the shop that stood on site.

EASTGATE SQUARE 1903 In this view can be seen the Eastgate Hand Laundry on the left, the Unicorn Public House and Light's Ironmongery: notice Mr. Lawrence, the milkman, on his rounds, in the foreground. The Gaumont Cinema was built on the site of the laundry in 1937 and was converted to a swimming pool in 1967.

84

EASTGATE SQUARE 1986 The old Unicorn was replaced by a new building which closed as a pub in 1962 and is now converted to offices. Lights became owned by Mr. Gilbert Pine. Pines the ironmongers are still in Eastgate Square in other premises. St.Pancras Church is the only feature still recognisable in the picture.

THE HORNET 1907 Johnny Grist was a well known Chichester character — he was a jobmaster who hired out horses and carriages. He was also a cowkeeper and also, later, the publican of the Prince Albert Inn, now the Bush, also in the Hornet.

THE HORNET 1986 Virtually unchanged, the shop, which is now an Artist's gallery, until recently housed Vivian Meynell's Bookshop on the upper floor, which gentleman was noted for serving coffee to browsing customers.

GREYFRIARS CHAPEL 1916 One of the most historic buildings in the city, Archbishop Peckham held an ordination there in 1282 when it was the Chapel of the Franciscan Friary. After the dissolution of the Monasteries in 1538 it became the Guildhall of the City Corporation. It was also used as The Court House for the Quarter Sessions.

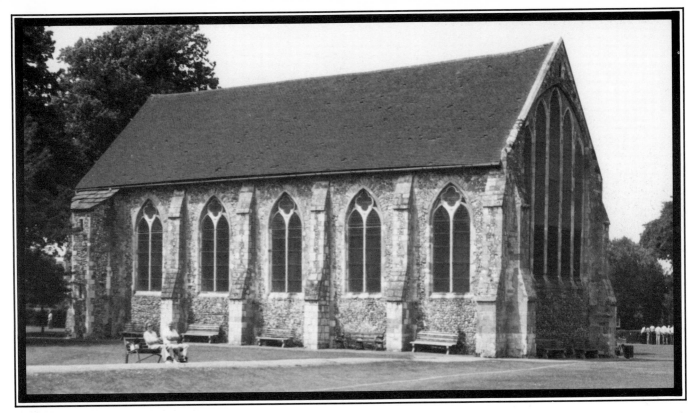

GREYFRIARS CHAPEL 1986 The jury room that was to be seen on the side of the chapel in the earlier photograph has been removed, in the meantime it had served as an armoury for the Sussex Rifle Volunteers. The building is now part of the Chichester District Museum, housing archaeological exhibits. It was visited by Her Majesty the Queen in 1956.

ST.PANCRAS 1970 In studying the pictures in this book one becomes aware of the cost to the city, in terms of lost buildings, caused by the construction of the Ring Road system. The cottages seen in this picture were among the last to go, their demolition was bitterly opposed by the Chichester Society and others, but to no avail.

ST.PANCRAS 1986 The new road that replaced the lost cottages were named Needlemakers, a tribute to the manufacturing industry that was centred in St Pancras during the 15th and 16th centuries.

SOMERSTOWN 1958 Somerstown was an area to the north of the city between Broyle Road and St Pauls Road. This picture taken in George Street shows Mants the Greengrocers and in the distance can be seen the Chichester Workhouse.

SOMERSTOWN 1986 Somerstown was demolished in 1960, the whole area was razed to the ground and the site stood empty for several years until the new Somerstown, seen here was built. The loss to the city was great, as it was not just the buildings but a whole community that had been dispersed.

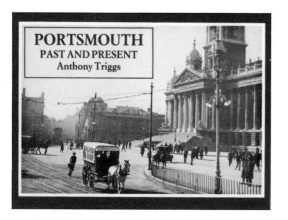
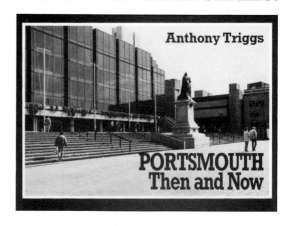

94

H.G.S.
Research Room